weblinks

You don't need a computer to use this book. But, for readers who do have access to the Internet, the book provides links to recommended websites which offer additional information and resources on the subject.

You will find weblinks boxes like this on some pages of the book.

weblinks

For more information about forces and motion, go to www.waylinks.co.uk /series/scienceinvestigations

waylinks.co.uk

To help you find the recommended websites easily and quickly, weblinks are provided on our own website, **waylinks.co.uk.** These take you straight to the relevant websites and save you typing in the Internet address yourself.

Internet safety

↗ Never give out personal details, which include: your name, address, school, telephone number, email address, password and mobile number.

↗ Do not respond to messages which make you feel uncomfortable – tell an adult.

↗ Do not arrange to meet in person someone you have met on the Internet.

↗ Never send your picture or anything else to an online friend without a parent's or teacher's permission.

↗ If you see anything that worries you, tell an adult.

A note to adults
Internet use by children should be supervised. We recommend that you install filtering software which blocks unsuitable material.

Website content

The weblinks for this book are checked and updated regularly. However, because of the nature of the Internet, the content of a website may change at any time, or a website may close down without notice. While the Publishers regret any inconvenience this may cause readers, they cannot be responsible for the content of any website other than their own.

WAYLAND

Science Investigations

FORCES AND MOTION

BY CHRIS OXLADE

WAYLAND

Titles in this series:

ELECTRICITY

FORCES AND MOTION

LIGHT

MAGNETISM

MATERIALS

SOUND

© 2006 Wayland

Produced for Wayland by
White-Thomson Publishing Ltd
210 High Street
Lewes, East Sussex
BN7 2NH

Editors: Sarah Doughty and Rachel Minay
Series design: Derek Lee
Book design: Malcolm Walker
Illustrator: Peter Bull
Text consultant: Dr Mike Goldsmith

Published in Great Britain in 2006 by Wayland,
an imprint of Hachette Children's Books.

Reprinted in 2007

British Library Cataloguing in Publication Data
    Oxlade, Chris
    Forces and Motion. – (Science Investigations)
    1. Force and energy - Juvenile literature 2. Motion - Juvenile literature
    I. Title
    531.1

ISBN 13: 978 0 7502 3478 8

Printed and bound in China.

Wayland
338 Euston Road, London NW1 3BH

The publishers would like to thank the following for permission to
reproduce these photographs:
Corbis: 4 right (Duomo), 9 (Phil Schermeister), 11 (Patrik Giardino), 12
(Simon Marcus), 16 (Jane Sapinsky), 21 (Karl Weatherly), Cover and 22
below (Paul Morris), 23 (Bettmann), 28 (Paul A. Souders); Ecoscene: 15
(Anthony Cooper); NASA Images: 7; OSF/Photolibrary: 4 left, 6 (Reso
E.E.I.G), 10 above and below, 13 (Index Stock Imagery), 17 (Don Johnston),
18 (Index Stock Imagery), 19 (Aflo Foto Agency), 20 (Johner Bildbyra), 26
(Index Stock Imagery), 27 (Mark Deeble & Victoria Stone), 29 (Mauritius Die
Bildagentur Gmbh); Science Photo Library: 14 (Detlev Van Ravenswaay), 24,
25 (Andrew Lambert Photography); Speedo International Limited, 2005: 22
above.

Contents

What are forces?

A force is simply a push or a pull. There are forces all around us, all the time. You use them to do everyday things, such as lift bags, open doors, and even walk along. Forces keep magnets stuck to your fridge door and you stuck to the earth! Forces can do many different things. Nothing starts moving or stops moving without a force making it start or stop. And when you stretch, squash or bend anything, you use forces to do it.

All forces have a size and a direction. So when you describe a force, you have to say how big it is and which way it is pushing or pulling. In diagrams we use arrows to show forces. The direction of the arrow shows which way the force is pushing or pulling. The length of an arrow is sometimes used to show the size of a force.

You use lots of different forces when you ride a bicycle. What forces do you use to make it turn a corner?

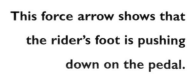

This force arrow shows that the rider's foot is pushing down on the pedal.

INVESTIGATION

What can forces do?

MATERIALS

A washing sponge.

INSTRUCTIONS

Put a washing sponge flat on a table. Use your fingers to make forces on the sponge. Try pushing just on one side. Then on the other side.

Try pushing on both sides. Try pulling on both sides.

You will see that different forces have different effects on the sponge.

FURTHER INVESTIGATION

Write down the different forces you tried using and what happened to the sponge in each case. Can you draw diagrams of the sponge with force arrows to show what forces you used?

Can you work out what forces would make the sponge spin?

weblinks
For more information about forces go to
www.waylinks.co.uk/series/ scienceinvestigations/forces

Why do things fall downwards?

weblinks

For more information about gravity go to www.waylinks.co.uk/series/scienceinvestigations/forces

EVIDENCE

Gravity is the force that pulls you and all the other objects on the earth down to the ground. It also makes objects such as balls fall back to earth when you throw them upwards. Gravity acts between the earth and every object. It tries to pull, or attract, objects to the earth, so it is called a force of attraction. If there were no force of gravity, everything on earth would float off into space and the earth itself would fall to pieces!

The force that you feel pulling an object down towards the ground is called its weight. Gravity pulls harder on objects with more matter in them, so the objects feel heavier.

When you jump or dive into a swimming pool, it's gravity that makes you fall into the water. Gravity tries to sink you, too!

Gravity exists on other planets, too, and on moons and the sun. The sun's gravity keeps the earth and the other planets moving around it. It stops them drifting away into space.

INVESTIGATION

How big is the force of gravity?

MATERIALS

An object that weighs about 500 g (such as a 500 ml bottle of drink), a strong elastic band and a ruler.

INSTRUCTIONS

This simple experiment will let you feel how much an object is attracted to the earth by gravity. Find an object that weighs 500 g. Tie a string around it and tie the other end of the string to a strong elastic band. Pick up the elastic band until the object is just lifted up. Measure the length of the band. Now untie the object and stretch the band until it is the same length as before. The pull you feel on your hands is the same as the force of attraction between the earth and the 500 g object. The earth is pulled towards the object with the same force as the object is pulled towards the earth.

On the moon, gravity is only about one sixth as strong as it is on earth. Could you jump higher on the moon than on earth?

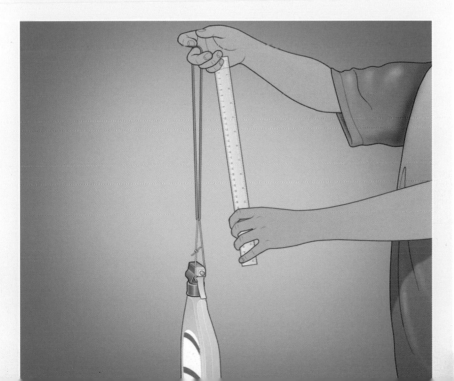

FURTHER INVESTIGATION

The pull of gravity from the moon pulls on the water in the earth's oceans. It makes the water slosh about slowly. What evidence is there of this at the seaside?

What makes magnets attract?

weblinks

For more information about magnetism go to www.waylinks.co.uk/series/scienceinvestigations/forces

EVIDENCE

A magnet, such as a fridge magnet, sticks to some metal objects, such as fridge doors and paper clips. This is because there is a magnetic force between the magnet and the metal. The force pulls the magnet and door together. It is a force of attraction.

A magnet has two places on it where the force is strongest. They are called its poles. One is called the north pole and the other is called the south pole. Both poles of a magnet attract pieces of metal. The opposite poles on two different magnets (a north pole and a south pole) attract each other, too. But two like poles on different magnets (two north poles or two south poles) push each other away instead. This is called a force of repulsion. So magnets can make both pulling and pushing forces.

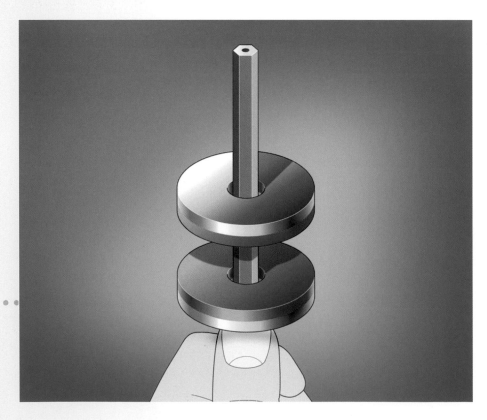

These are ring magnets. The top one floats because the two magnets repel. What poles are facing each other?

8

INVESTIGATION

How strong is the magnetic force?

MATERIALS

Two bar magnets.

INSTRUCTIONS

Lay both magnets on a desk top a few centimetres apart. Turn them so that two opposite poles (a north pole and a south pole) are pointing at each other. Slide the magnets slowly towards each other. At first there is no attraction, but you can feel the force increase quickly as the magnets get closer together.

Now turn the magnets so that two like poles are pointing at each other. Move them together again and feel the force. The magnetic force is only strong when the magnets are very close together.

FURTHER INVESTIGATION

A compass needle is a small magnet. Its poles are attracted and repelled by the earth, which acts like a huge bar magnet. Suspend a bar magnet on a cotton thread. The north pole will point towards 'magnetic north' on the earth.

These boys on a walking trip are learning how to find their way using a map and compass. Sailors also use a compass for navigation. How does it help them?

What happens when you squash a spring?

The boy in this picture is bouncing on a pogo stick, a toy that has a huge spring. What does the spring do when it is squashed down?

weblinks

For more information about forces on objects go to www.waylinks.co.uk/series/scienceinvestigations/forces

Springs on a mountain bike let the wheels bounce up and down over bumps.

EVIDENCE

If you push on the two ends of a metal spring (such as the spring from a pen) the spring pushes back on your fingers with a force. It tries to push your fingers apart again. The opposite happens when you pull on the ends of a spring. The spring pulls back on your fingers with a force. It tries to pull your fingers back together again. The bigger the force you use to squash or stretch a spring, the bigger the force the spring pushes or pulls back with.

All objects squash and stretch like springs. But normally they only squash and stretch a very tiny amount, so you can't see it happening. The tiny particles inside the object are squeezed together or pulled apart. They always try to push apart again or pull together again to make the object return to shape.

INVESTIGATION

How strong is the force in an elastic band?

MATERIALS

A selection of elastic bands, some thick and some thin, but all around the same length.

INSTRUCTIONS

Stretch a thin band between your hands. Can you feel that the more you stretch the band, the more it tries to pull your hands together again? Now try the same thing with a thicker band. The band is more difficult to stretch because it makes a bigger force. Try with two or three bands together.

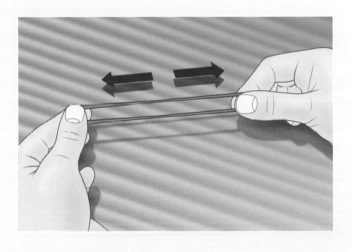

FURTHER INVESTIGATION

Bending an object makes one part of the object stretch and another part squash. The object tries to return to shape. Try bending a thin piece of wood to feel this springy effect.

• • • • • • • • • • • • • •

This diver is preparing to dive from a springboard. What does the board do to help her dive?

Why do things start moving?

weblinks

For more information about forces and movement go to www.waylinks.co.uk/series/scienceinvestigations/forces

You push a person on a swing to get them moving. Can you work out what force makes the person swing back to you again?

EVIDENCE

Things don't just start moving on their own. They need a force to make them move. For example, you need to push on a sledge or a toy car to get it going. The object always starts to move in the same direction as the force you make. So when you push on the back of a sledge, it moves forwards. The bigger the force on an object, the more quickly it starts moving.

As long as a force pushes on an object, the object gets faster and faster. So if you keep pushing on a sledge along a flat surface, it keeps speeding up. This is called accelerating. When you stop pushing a sledge, it keeps moving, but it does not speed up anymore.

The heavier an object is, the bigger the force needed to get it going. So a trolley full of shopping is harder to start off than one that's empty.

A heavy freight train like this
one needs two locomotives
pulling to get it moving.

INVESTIGATION

How does the size of a force change the speed of an object?

MATERIALS

A sheet of card, marbles, a ruler, a stopwatch
and a felt-tip pen.

INSTRUCTIONS

Put a sheet of card on a smooth floor. Make
marks on the card, every 5 cm from the
bottom and prop up one end to make a
ramp. Also make a mark on the floor 50 cm
from the bottom of the ramp. Now put a
marble at the bottom mark and let it roll.
Use a stopwatch or the second hand of an
ordinary watch to measure how long it takes
to get from the bottom of the ramp to the
mark on the floor. Try again from the other
marks on the ramp.

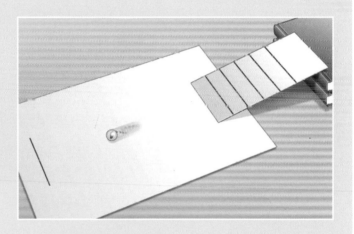

Gravity pulls the marble down the ramp. The
longer gravity pulls on the marble, the faster
it gets, so the quicker it rolls along the floor.

FURTHER INVESTIGATION

Write down the distance up the ramp and
the time in a table. Now draw a line graph with
the distance along the bottom and the time up
the side. What shape of line did you get?

Why do things stop moving?

This picture shows the Mars Polar Lander, a lightweight spacecraft, on its way to Mars. There is nothing to slow down a spacecraft, so it keeps going forever without needing its engines.

We know that things don't start moving on their own. Well, they don't slow down or stop moving on their own either! They need a force to slow or stop them. If there's no force, they keep going forever.

To slow down an object you have to make a force in the opposite direction to the way the object is moving. Imagine a sledge that is sliding towards you – you have to push on its front to slow it. You have to pull back on the handle of a shopping trolley to slow it. If you keep pulling on the handles the trolley keeps slowing down and finally comes to a stop.

The heavier an object is, the bigger the force that is needed to slow it down or stop it. So you have to pull harder to stop a full trolley than an empty one.

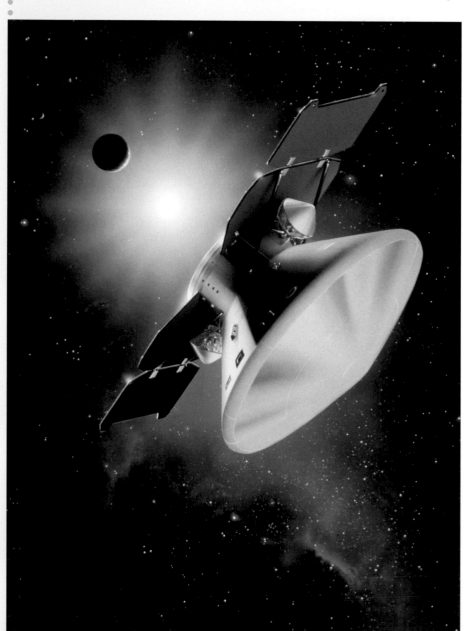

weblinks
For information about crash testing go to
www.waylinks.co.uk/series/
scienceinvestigations/forces

INVESTIGATION

How long does it take a force to slow an object?

MATERIALS

A large metal paper clip, thin elastic bands and a marble.

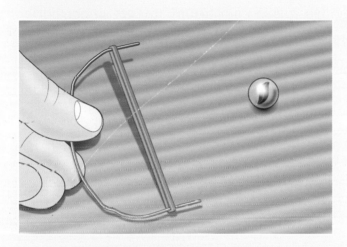

INSTRUCTIONS

Unbend a paper clip to make a U shape. Stretch a thin elastic band across the ends of the U, about 1 cm from the ends of the wire. Hold the wire horizontally and roll a marble at the elastic band. As the marble hits the band, the band will stretch. The band makes a force that slows the marble to a stop, then pushes it back the other way. Roll the marble at different speeds and watch how far the band bends.

These barriers in the centre of a motorway bend when cars hit them. Why is this better than having a solid wall?

FURTHER INVESTIGATION

Can you find any examples where springs and other devices are used to bring objects to a stop slowly instead of with a bump?

What do two forces do?

weblinks

For more information about the result of forces on a body go to **www.waylinks.co.uk/series/scienceinvestigations/forces**

A floating object, like this toy boat, is in equilibrium. It is pushed upwards by the water. There must also be a force the same size in the opposite direction. What is it?

These force arrows show that the two forces on a floating object are equal but opposite.

When you push or pull on one side of an object, the object begins to move to one side or the other. But if you push with the same force on both sides of an object, the object stays where it is.

The two forces are the same size, but they push in opposite directions, so they cancel each other out. The object does not move, so we say that it is in equilibrium. You are in equilibrium most of your life! When you are standing still, gravity is pulling you down and the ground is pushing you up (you can feel this force on the soles of your feet). The two forces cancel each other out, so you don't move up or down!

Two forces often cause an object to stretch or squash. For example, you can squash a ball of modelling clay by pressing it on both sides.

INVESTIGATION

When do forces become balanced?

MATERIALS

A block of wood and a bowl of water.

INSTRUCTIONS

Fill a bowl with water. Put a block of wood into the water so that it floats. The wood is in equilibrium. Its weight pulls it down and the water pushes it up with a force the same size. Push the wood under the water and let go. The wood is not in equilibrium now. The force pushing up is greater than its weight. Overall the force on the block is upwards, so it bobs up again.

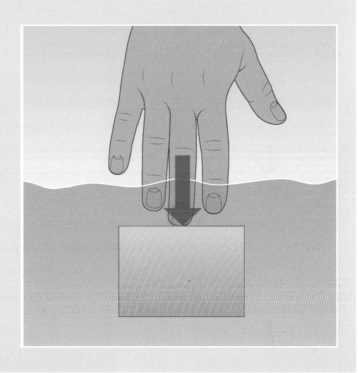

FURTHER INVESTIGATION

Two forces can also make an object turn round. Put your block of wood on a table and try to make it spin on the spot. What forces do you have to use?

A driver turns a steering wheel with two hands. What forces are the driver's hands making?

Why do things move in circles?

weblinks

For more information about what keeps a satellite in orbit go to **www.waylinks.co.uk/series/ scienceinvestigations/forces**

EVIDENCE

What makes you go round on a roundabout or a train go round a curved track? The answer is a force. We know that things stay still or keep moving at the same speed unless a force makes them speed up or slow down. They also keep going in a straight line unless a force pushes or pulls on them.

A force pushing on one side of a moving object makes the object change direction. If the force only pushes for a short time the object turns slightly. For example, railway tracks push a train's wheels sideways, making the train go round a curve. If a force carries on pushing on the side of an object, the object keeps changing direction. In the end it goes round in a circle! For example, when you are on a roundabout, the seat pushes you towards the middle of the roundabout all the time. This push makes you go round in a circle.

This picture shows a satellite in orbit. The force of gravity makes it go in a huge circle around the earth.

18

INVESTIGATION

What force makes a weight on a string go round?

MATERIALS

String and a heavy key.

INSTRUCTIONS

Go outside in an open space. Tie the key firmly to the end of a 30 cm piece of string. Hold the other end of the string between your finger and thumb.

With your other hand throw the key so that it goes in a circle on the end of the string. Can you feel the force on your fingers as the key goes round? This is because your hand is making the force on the string that keeps the key moving in a circle.

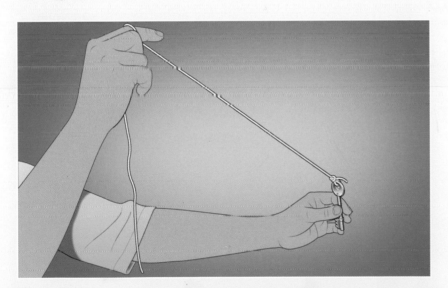

This hammer thrower is whirling the hammer very fast. What happens when she lets go?

(F)URTHER INVESTIGATION

Make the key go round again. Now let go of the string. What happens to the key? Why does it go off in a straight line?

What force slows things down?

You know that things don't slow down unless a force makes them slow down. So if you slide a pen across a desk, why does it soon slow down and stop? What is the force that stops it? The answer is friction.

Friction is a force that happens between two objects that touch each other. It tries to stop the objects, such as the pen and the desk, sliding past each other. The size of friction is bigger when the surfaces of the objects are rough.

Sometimes friction is useful. For example, friction between your shoes and the ground stops your feet sliding about when you walk. Sometimes friction is a problem. In machines, it tries to stop the machine's parts moving past each other. Putting oil on the parts helps because it reduces friction.

weblinks
For more information about friction go to
www.waylinks.co.uk/series/ scienceinvestigations/forces

A barrow makes it easier to move a heavy load. Can you think why?

Putting oil on moving parts – for example, oiling a bicycle chain – is called lubrication. It reduces friction and helps to stop the parts wearing out.

INVESTIGATION

What makes friction bigger or smaller?

MATERIALS

A small cardboard box, a sheet of paper and some small books.

INSTRUCTIONS

Stand a small cardboard box on a flat table top. Push it slowly along. How much friction tries to stop the box moving? Now put a book on top of the box and try again. Add more books and try again. You should find that the heavier the box, the more friction there is. This is because the base of the box presses harder on the table.

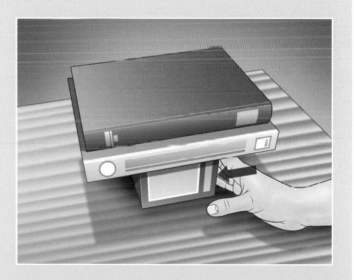

FURTHER INVESTIGATION

Now put a sheet of smooth paper between the box and the table. Try pushing the box again. Does friction decrease this time? Why do you think that is?

How does air slow things down?

Some swimming racers wear a special swimsuit that makes less drag than their skin would.

Even if you keep the wheels of your bicycle oiled, the bicycle still slows down when you stop pedalling. This is because of another force that, like friction, tries to slow down moving things. It is called drag, or air resistance. Drag is made by the air. It happens because objects moving through the air have to push the air out of the way. Drag happens in water, too, but it is much bigger than in the air. So drag in water makes you come to a stop very quickly if you stop swimming.

The faster you go on your bicycle, the bigger the drag gets. Eventually it gets so big that you can't go any faster, no matter how hard you pedal. The drag on an object can be made smaller by making the object a smoother shape. This lets the air flow smoothly round it.

These cyclists are wearing crash helmets and close-fitting clothes to make themselves a smoother shape. What else are they doing to reduce drag?

22

INVESTIGATION

What shapes make most drag?

MATERIALS

Thin card, a stapler and a hairdryer.

INSTRUCTIONS

Make a square tube, a round tube and a fish-shaped tube from strips of card. Staple the sides together. Try to make each shape about the same size. Stand the shapes on a table. Move a hairdryer towards the front of each one in turn. Which shape can you get closest to before it slides backwards in the moving air? Which one makes the least drag?

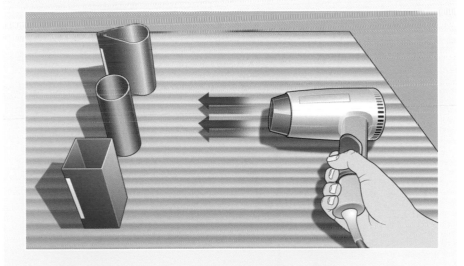

Why does a parachutist quickly slow down when the parachute opens?

FURTHER INVESTIGATION

Sometimes it is useful to increase the drag on an object on purpose. Can you think of any examples?

weblinks

For more information about drag go to
www.waylinks.co.uk/series/
scienceinvestigations/forces

23

How do we measure forces?

Scientists and engineers often need to measure the size of a force. For example, when engineers are designing a bridge, they need to work out the forces that will press on it so that they can work out how strong to make the bridge. The size of a force is measured in units called newtons. A force of one newton is about the same as the force of gravity on a 100 g object.

We measure force by looking at the effect the force has on something. The simplest device for measuring force is called a forcemeter. The stronger the force on the spring, the further it stretches. The amount it stretches shows how big the force is. A weighing machine measures the force of gravity on an object. It is a special type of force-measuring machine.

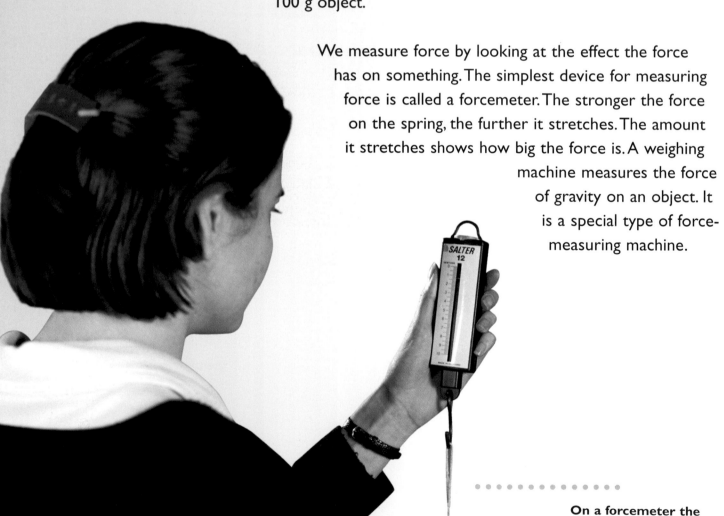

On a forcemeter the pointer moves down the scale to indicate the force in newtons.

When we need to weigh things very accurately, we use electronic scales like these. A tiny crystal inside makes electricity when it is squashed by the weight of the object on the scales. The heavier the weight, the more electricity is produced.

INVESTIGATION

How can elastic bands measure force?

MATERIALS
Thick card, a thin elastic band, paper clips and string.

INSTRUCTIONS
Cut a piece of thick card three times as long as your elastic band. Cut two slots in one end of the card and slot the elastic band in. Attach a paper clip to the other end of the elastic band. Pull the band straight and make a mark on the card at the end of the paper clip. Write 0 next to it. Make a mark every 1 cm to the end of the card. Write 1, 2, 3, etc. next to these marks.

Hang an object on the paper clip. The heavier the object, the greater the force shown on the scale.

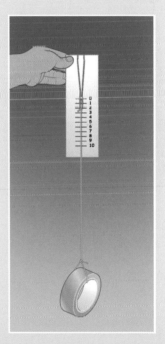

FURTHER INVESTIGATION

Use the force-measuring device to measure the size of the force of friction in the experiment on page 21. Pull the box with a string attached to the box and the paper clip.

What is pressure?

weblinks

Learn how to make a pen cap 'submarine' at
**www.waylinks.co.uk/series/
scienceinvestigations/forces**

EVIDENCE

Pressure is the amount of force that presses on a particular area. The bigger the force or the smaller the area, the bigger the pressure is. For example, the pressure on your toes is different when you're standing normally and when you're standing on tiptoe. When you are standing normally, your weight is spread over the whole bottom of your foot. This means that the pressure on each small area of your foot, such as the bottoms of your toes, is quite small. But if you stand on tiptoe, all your weight is on your toes. So the same force (which is your weight) is spread over a much smaller area than before. The pressure is higher and it quickly begins to hurt!

It is often useful to reduce pressure. This truck has lots of tyres so it does not damage the road surface. How does this reduce pressure?

26

INVESTIGATION

How can you change pressure?

MATERIALS

A brick, marbles, an old tray and sand.

INSTRUCTIONS

Fill an old tray with sand until the sand is a few centimetres deep. Level the top of the sand to make a smooth, flat surface. Put a brick on top of the sand. Does the brick sink in? It just leaves a tiny mark because the pressure on the sand is low. Now put four marbles on the sand and rest the brick on them. The marbles sink into the sand because the weight of the brick is now on a much smaller area. The pressure on the sand is much higher.

Pressure happens underwater, too. This submersible needs a strong hull in order not to be crushed by the pressure of the water around it when it is deep down in the ocean.

FURTHER INVESTIGATION

Put some warm water inside an empty soft drink bottle. Swirl it round to warm the bottle and the air inside. Empty the water out and put the lid on tightly. Why does the bottle gradually get crushed?

How do we make forces bigger?

weblinks

For more information about simple machines go to www.waylinks.co.uk/series/scienceinvestigations/forces

EVIDENCE

We often need to move an object or change its shape, but on our own we cannot make enough force to do it. Somehow we need to make the force from our hands bigger. We can do this with a simple machine.

For example, you use nutcrackers to crack the shell of a nut that is too tough to crack by squeezing with your hands. Nutcrackers are a simple machine. They are made up of two rods called levers, joined together at a pivot. Pressing the handles together with a small force makes the levers squeeze the nut with a much greater force.

Tools such as pliers and scissors, and kitchen gadgets such as tin openers, use levers, too. Another simple machine is the pulley, which makes it easier to lift heavy objects.

This digger is using pulleys to make lifting easier.

INVESTIGATION

How can one coin balance two?

MATERIALS

A ruler, heavy coins and a pencil.

INSTRUCTIONS

Put a ruler flat on a table and put a pencil under its centre so that the ruler balances. The ruler acts as a lever and the pencil acts as its pivot. Put two coins halfway between the pivot and one end of the ruler. The weight of the coins will make the lever unbalanced. Now see if you can balance the lever by putting one coin on the other side of the pivot. Can you see how the lever allows the small weight of one coin to lift the larger weight of two coins?

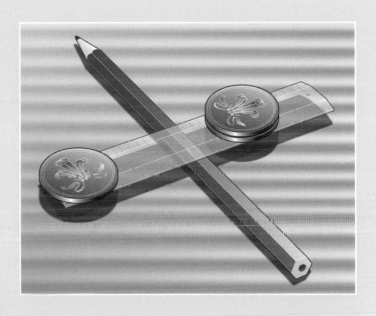

FURTHER INVESTIGATION

Find a picture of a tower construction crane. Look for a large weight on the crane. What do you think it does?

This weighing machine is called a beam balance. The beam is a lever. It is tipped one way or the other by weights in the pans.

Glossary

Attraction
A force that tries to pull two objects towards each other.

Compass
A device used to help find direction. The thin needle inside the compass always points north.

Drag
A force that tries to stop objects moving through the air or through water. It is made by the air or water.

Electromagnet
A magnet made by electricity. A simple electromagnet is made up of wire carrying electricity wound up to make a coil.

Equilibrium
When an object has two or more forces pushing or pulling on it that cancel each other out.

Force
A push or a pull.

Freight
Things carried by a train, truck or ship.

Friction
A force that tries to stop two things that are touching sliding past each other.

Gravity
The force that pulls things towards the sun, earth or other large object.

Lever
A bar or a rod that makes a force bigger or smaller. It is a simple machine. A lever is always fixed at one place called the pivot, but it can turn around the pivot.

Locomotive
A machine that pulls carriages or wagons on a railway.

Machine
A device for carrying out tasks. Levers and pulleys are simple machines.

Magnet
A piece of material that attracts iron and steel objects. The material is said to be magnetic.

Pivot
The place where a lever turns around.

Pole
One of the places on a magnet where the force of magnetism is strongest. All magnets have two poles.

Pressure
The amount of force on a certain area.

Pulley
A simple machine that makes it easier to lift heavy objects.

Repulsion
A force that tries to push two objects away from each other.

Submersible
A machine like a mini submarine, used to explore under the water.

Weight
The downwards force on an object made by gravity.

Further information

BOOKS

Fascinating Forces: The Wonderful World of Forces and Movement (Shooting Stars)
by Robert Roland
(Belitha Press Ltd, 2002)

Forces (Factfinders)
by Chris Oxlade
(BBC Books, 1995)

Forces (Science Experiments)
by Sally Nankivell-Aston and Dot Jackson
(Franklin Watts, 2000)

Forces and Motion (Science Files)
by Chris Oxlade
(Hodder Wayland, 2005)

Forces and Motion (Science Files)
by Steve Parker
(Heinemann Library, 2004)

Forces and Motion (Science, the Facts)
by Rebecca Hunter
(Franklin Watts, 2003)

Forces and Motion: From Push to Shove
(Science Answers)
by Christopher Cooper
(Heinemann Library, 2003)

Hands-on Science
by Sarah Angliss, Jack Challoner, John Graham and Peter Mellett
(Kingfisher Books, 2002)

The Spark Files: Dark Forces
by Terry Deary and Barbara Allen
(Faber and Faber, 1999)

Under Pressure: Forces (Everyday Science)
by Ann Fullick
(Heinemann Library, 2004)

CD-ROMS

Seeing Science: Forces
(4Learning)

ANSWERS

Page 4 You push on one handlebar and pull on the other.

Page 5 Pushing in opposite directions on two corners of the sponge, but not towards the centre of the sponge, would make it spin round.

Page 7 The tide goes in and out as the water level rises and falls.

Yes, you could jump six times as high!

Page 8 Two like poles are facing each other (either two north poles or two south poles).

Page 9 The magnetized needle in a compass always points in the same direction. This allows a walker or sailor to work out which way they are travelling.

Page 10 The spring pushes the rider upwards.

Page 11 A springboard springs back into a straight position, helping the diver to jump into the air.

Page 12 The force of gravity makes the person swing back down again. It's also gravity that slows them as they swing upwards again.

Page 15 When the barriers bend, they work a bit like springs. They bring cars to a stop more slowly than a solid wall, which would stop cars instantly. Stopping more slowly helps to reduce injuries to passengers.

Page 16 The second force is gravity pulling the boat downwards.

Page 17 You have to use two forces in opposite directions, but not along the same line, otherwise they cancel out.

To turn a wheel, you push up on one side and down on the other.

Page 19 The key goes in a straight line because the force making it go in a circle has been removed.

The force making the hammer go in a circle is removed, so it flies away in a straight line.

Page 20 The barrow's wheel reduces friction.

Page 21 The sheet of paper has a smooth surface that reduces friction.

Page 22 Each cyclist is leaning forwards, which makes his body a more streamlined shape, and so reduces drag.

Page 23 A parachute makes lots more drag than the parachutist's body. When it opens it makes an upwards pull on the parachutist, slowing him or her down.

Two examples are air brakes on aircraft and parachutes to slow landing jet fighters.

Page 26 The more tyres a truck has, the bigger the area of tyre that touches the road, and the less the pressure on the road.

Page 27 As the air inside the bottle cools, its pressure goes down. The air pressure on the outside of the bottle crushes it.

Page 29 The crane's arm is like a lever. The weight balances the weight of the object the crane lifts.

Index